GET A REACTION

Experiments with Mixtures, Solutions, & Reactions

NICK ARNOLD

Quarto Library

Quarto Knows

Quarto is the authority on a wide range of topics.

Quarto educates, entertains and enriches the lives of our readers—enthusiasts and lovers of hands-on living.

www.quartoknows.com

Publisher: Maxime Boucknooghe
Editorial Director: Victoria Garrard
Art Director: Miranda Snow
Project editor: Sophie Hallam
Design and Editorial: Cloud King Creative
Consultant: Pete Robinson
CSciTeach of the Association for Science Education

This library edition published in 2019 by Quarto Library,
an imprint of The Quarto Group.
6 Orchard Road, Suite 100
Lake Forest, CA 92630
T: +1 949 380 7510
F: +1 949 380 7575
www.QuartoKnows.com

A CIP record for this book is available from the Library of Congress.

ISBN 978 0 71124 226 5

Manufactured in Dongguan, China TL012019

9 8 7 6 5 4 3 2 1

FSC www.fsc.org
MIX
Paper from responsible sources
FSC® C104723

CONTENTS

THE THREE RULES OF EXPERIMENTING

All great scientists know the three golden rules of experimenting. These rules show you how to experiment safely and happily.

RULE #1

BE ORGANIZED

Before you start the experiment, read the WHAT YOU NEED list of materials and equipment. Make sure you have everything you need. If you go off in search of something halfway through an experiment, it may not be safe and it might ruin your results. If you can't find what you need, feel free to use a similar item, but ALWAYS ask before you borrow anything!

RULE #2

BE SAFE

This is a book for safe scientists. Adult supervision is always needed with experiments. Pay attention to all the DANGER warnings. In particular, NEVER drink or eat an experiment unless this book says you can.

- BEWARE of hot water.
- BEWARE of hot sugar.
- BEWARE of handling ice—always wear gloves.

This book doesn't need mains electricity, fire, or harmful chemicals—so don't use them in your experiments!

RULE #3

BE CLEAN

Be careful not to spill messy materials like water or food coloring. Always clean up before you start a new experiment. Cleaning up sounds seriously boring, but it helps you. Yes, really! Cleaning up:

- Clears space for your next experiment.
- Keeps you from losing vital equipment.
- Keeps younger kids from playing with your experiments and hurting themselves or breaking your equipment.
- Means you won't get grounded and banned from experimenting!

WHAT'S NEXT?

Look out for the "What's Next?" challenge. Search for clues to explore and develop the experiments in the book—and find the answers for yourselves! See if you can set up your own lab area at home, with a box for your lab equipment. You could keep a notebook with the results of your experiments.

EDIBLE GAS

Did you know that it's possible to make your own edible air? Try this experiment to give your mouth a tasty treat!

WHAT YOU NEED

- Magnifying glass
- ½ cup sugar
- 4 teaspoons of water
- Measuring cup
- Saucepan
- Baking powder
- Teaspoon
- Aluminum foil
- Margarine
- Roasting pan

WHAT YOU DO

1. Line the roasting pan with aluminum foil and grease with margarine. Place the roasting pan in the fridge for 30 minutes.
2. An adult should heat the sugar and two teaspoons of water in the saucepan. The sugar turns runny, then dry, and then brown. When the mixture turns brown, add another two teaspoons of water.
3. When the sugar starts to bubble, an adult should add a teaspoon of baking powder. They need to stir the mixture well.
4. Now pour the mixture into the roasting pan.
5. Allow the mixture to cool. Hold it to the light and examine with a magnifying glass.

QUIZ QUESTION:

WHERE DO THE BUBBLES COME FROM?

A) BOILING SUGAR AND WATER

B) A CHEMICAL REACTION CAUSED BY BAKING POWDER

C) SOMEONE MUST HAVE DROOLED IN MY EXPERIMENT

WHAT HAPPENS?

ANSWER: B

Baking powder reacts with water to make carbon dioxide gas. The gooey cooling sugar traps air bubbles made by the gas.

WARNING!

BEWARE OF HEAT. ADULT HELP IS VITAL! A GROWN-UP CAN CLEAN THE SAUCEPAN BY BOILING WATER IN IT.

THE ACID TEST

Vinegar is slightly acidic and tastes tingly on your tongue. But is it possible to test acid without actually tasting it?

WHAT YOU NEED

WHAT YOU DO

1. Pour ½ cup of grape juice into the first glass and then rinse out the measuring cup.
2. Pour ¼ cup of lemon juice into the second glass. Stir in ¼ cup of grape juice. Rinse out the measuring cup again.
3. Add ¼ cup of water to the third glass and stir in one heaping teaspoon of baking powder. Stir regularly until the mixture no longer fizzes when stirred.
4. Add ¼ cup of grape juice to the third glass and stir again.
5. Compare the color of each liquid.

QUIZ QUESTION:

WHAT WILL HAPPEN TO THE COLORS?

A) THE COLORS IN THE LIQUIDS MIX TO MAKE NEW COLORS

B) STIRRING THE JUICE CHANGES ITS COLOR

C) THERE'S A CHEMICAL REACTION AFFECTING THE COLOR

WHAT HAPPENS?

ANSWER: C

The lemon juice turns the grape juice pinkish (2) and the baking powder turns the grape juice purplish (3). The grape juice glass reminds you of the original color (1). This is called a control.

Acids and alkalis alter color molecules in the juice. Baking powder is a type of base called an alkali, and lemon juice contains an acid.

DID YOU KNOW?

A substance that changes color with acid or alkali is called an **indicator**. Other vegetable dyes such as beetroot juice and red cabbage juice also work as indicators.

CONTROL (GRAPE JUICE) — WITH LEMON JUICE — WITH BAKING POWDER

CRAZY COLORS

Science can be colorful and even artistic. This simple experiment shows you how to turn milk into something pretty.

WHAT YOU DO

1. Cover the bowl base with milk.
2. Place droplets of food coloring in the milk. Space the drops out.
3. Dip the cotton swab into the dish soap.
4. Touch the milk with the cotton swab.

WHAT YOU NEED

Whole milk

Dish soap

Bowl

Cotton swab

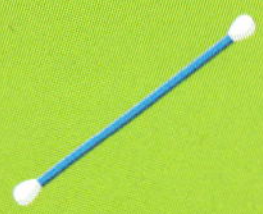

Liquid food coloring (not gel)

Use as many colors as you like!

QUIZ QUESTION:

WHAT WILL THE COLORS DO?

A) BUBBLE AND FLOAT UP TO THE CEILING

B) MAKE SWIRLING PATTERNS

C) FORM STRIPES

WHAT HAPPENS?

ANSWER: B

The detergent in the soap breaks down **surface tension**, allowing the water and fat droplets in the milk to mix. As they mix, you see swirls in the food coloring.

The detergent molecules help water molecules and fat molecules join together. The fat molecules are very large and have to twist and move around to join with the detergent molecules. This swirls the food coloring around.

DID YOU KNOW?

In ancient Roman times, detergents were soaps made by mixing fat and ash!

OILY LAVA LAMP

This experiment isn't really a lamp, but thanks to clever chemistry, it looks just like one.

WHAT YOU NEED

- Vegetable oil
- Glass of warm water
- Liquid food coloring
- Salt
- Flashlight
- Teaspoon

WHAT YOU DO

1. Add liquid food coloring to the water and stir in well.
2. Pour the vegetable oil onto the surface of the water in a layer that's more than ¼ inch thick.
3. Now sprinkle a spoonful of salt onto the oil. Watch what happens and then add more salt.

QUIZ QUESTION:

WHAT WILL HAPPEN TO THE OIL?

A) GLOWS IN THE DARK

B) STARTS TO SMELL BAD

C) SINKS AND THEN RISES

WHAT HAPPENS?

ANSWER: C

Oil floats because it's less dense than water. The salt grains drag oil to the bottom of the glass. Oil bubbles rise as the salt **dissolves** in water.

WHAT'S NEXT?

Darken the room and shine a flashlight through the glass. It looks just like a lava lamp!

DID YOU KNOW?

Oil and water don't mix because water molecules are more attracted to each other than to the oil molecules.

MAKE BUTTER

How delicious is melted butter on hot toast? Yum! But what's the yellow stuff made of, and how is it made?

WHAT YOU DO

1. Allow the heavy cream to stand at room temperature for 1 hour.
2. Ask an adult to use a blender to blend the cream. The heavy cream will thicken and turn crumbly. White liquid will soon appear. Stop blending when there's no more white liquid being produced.
3. Collect the yellow solids in a strainer. Over a bowl, squeeze the yellow solids between the two large spoons to wring out any more liquid.
4. The yellow stuff is butter. Fill another bowl with water, then add the ice and butter. Gently press out more liquid from the butter between the spoons into the surrounding water. The butter will turn crumbly. Sift the butter from the bowl and press it into the third bowl. Squeeze out the liquid one last time. Store your butter in the fridge.

QUIZ QUESTION:

WHY WILL BLENDING THE MIXTURE MAKE BUTTER?

A) IT ALLOWS TINY BLOBS OF FAT TO CONNECT

B) IT TRIGGERS A CHEMICAL REACTION THAT BREAKS UP CREAM

C) IT MAKES CERTAIN CREAM CHEMICALS CHANGE COLOR

WHAT HAPPENS?

ANSWER: A

Cream is water with microscopic balls of fat. The fat balls have walls that stop them from merging. Shaking breaks the walls. The fat balls clump together to make butter.

WHAT'S NEXT?

Butter has the same **density** as ice. How can you prove this at Step 4?

WHAT YOU NEED

2 large spoons

½ pint of heavy cream

Blender

3 large bowls

Ice cubes

Strainer

DID YOU KNOW?

In Africa and the Middle East, it is traditional to make butter by rocking milk in a goatskin bag.

MAKE PLASTIC

So far we've had science experiments you can eat and drink. Now here's how to make plastic in your very own kitchen!

WHAT YOU DO

1. Ask an adult to heat the milk in a saucepan until it starts to simmer.
2. The adult should then pour the milk into the bowl.
3. Stir in 4 teaspoonfuls of vinegar. White lumps will form.
4. Sift out the white lumps. Rinse the lumps in water and press them together in a clean cloth or paper towel.

QUIZ QUESTION:

WHAT WOULD HAPPEN IF YOU USED A DIFFERENT ACID SUCH AS LEMON JUICE?

A) THE MILK WOULD STILL FORM LUMPS

B) NO LUMPS FORM

C) THE LEMON JUICE WOULD MAKE THE MILK TURN YELLOW

WHAT HAPPENS?

ANSWER: A

Milk contains casein molecules. Casein is found in cheese. The molecule is normally rolled into tight balls, but the acid makes it unravel like string.

The stringy molecules form lumps. All plastics are made of long molecules called **polymers** that are easy to mold.

WHAT'S NEXT?

Try adding food coloring to the milk after warming, but before adding the vinegar.

DID YOU KNOW?

Before 1945, milk casein was often used to make plastic. The plastic was made into buttons or jewellery!

WHAT YOU NEED

MIXTURES QUIZ

1) WHICH SUBSTANCE CONTAINS A BASE?

2) WHICH SUBSTANCE CONTAINS AN ACID?

3) WHICH THREE SUBSTANCES CAN YOU MIX TO MAKE CARBON DIOXIDE?

A Water
B Sugar
C Vinegar
D Salt
E Baking soda
F Cheese

Answers: 1) E, 2) C, 3) A, C, E.

MAKE IT RAIN

With the help of science, you can make it rain!

WHAT YOU DO

1. Wear gloves and cover the base of the metal bowl with ice. Leave the bowl in the freezer for a few hours.
2. Ask an adult helper to boil a pot of water and then allow it to cool down for 2–3 minutes.
3. Fill the clear bowl halfway with hot water and stir in one teaspoonful of salt. Dip the teaspoon in the water and taste it. The water should taste salty.
4. Wear gloves and place the metal bowl over the clear bowl. "Rain" will fall from the metal bowl into the water. Use the spoon to collect and taste the water.

WARNING!
BOILING WATER CAN BE DANGEROUS. ICE CAN BURN SKIN—ALWAYS WEAR GLOVES WHEN TOUCHING ICE OR COLD METAL.

QUIZ QUESTION:

DOES THE "RAIN" TASTE SALTY?

A) YES—IT CAME FROM SALTY WATER

B) NO—IT'S MADE OF WATER ONLY

C) YES—BUT LESS SALTY THAN WATER IN THE GLASS BOWL

WHAT HAPPENS?

ANSWER: B

The salt and water bond to form a solution. As the water is heated, the water molecules gain enough energy to break free and float into the air, forming a gas called water vapor. This process is called evaporation.

Water in the bowl evaporates. When the water vapor touches the cold metal, it condenses into water (this process is called condensation). Salt does not evaporate, so the water doesn't taste salty.

WHAT YOU NEED

Ice cubes

Gloves

A large, clear bowl

Teaspoon

Salt

Metal bowl or plate large enough to cover the bowl

Soup spoon

DID YOU KNOW?

Evaporation and condensation create weather. Clouds are formed from water vapor from lakes and seas. As the clouds cool, the water vapor condenses into droplets. That's where rain comes from!

POP BAG

This is a messy experiment that's guaranteed to go off with a bang!

WHAT YOU NEED

WHAT YOU DO

1. Heap 1½ tablespoons of baking soda on a sheet of paper towel. Fold the paper around the powder to form a small packet.
2. Mix ½ cup of vinegar in the measuring cup with ⅓ cup of warm water. Take the plastic bag outside and pour the mixture into it.
3. Drop the baking soda packet into the plastic bag and quickly seal it up.
4. Shake the bag as fast as you can, then drop the bag, stand back and enjoy the show!

QUIZ QUESTION:

WHAT DO YOU THINK WILL HAPPEN TO THE BAG?

A) THE BAG FILLS WITH GAS AND WATER UNTIL IT BURSTS

B) THE BAG HEATS UP—THIS INCREASES AIR PRESSURE

C) PAPER TOWEL EXPLODES WHEN MIXED WITH BAKING SODA

WHAT HAPPENS?

ANSWER: A

This experiment is a chemical reaction. That's when **atoms** or molecules combine to form new molecules.

The baking soda reacts with the acid in the vinegar, creating more water and carbon dioxide gas. The carbon dioxide gas fills the bag until it pops.

WHAT'S NEXT?

Try the experiment with more or less baking soda. Will it work if you leave out the water?

DID YOU KNOW?

Baking soda is an ingredient of natron. This was the substance used to dry out Egyptian mummies!

MAKE PEANUT BUTTER

Here's a fantastic edible experiment that's tasty AND scientific!

WHAT YOU NEED

- 1½ tablespoons of sunflower oil
- 1½ tablespoons of honey
- Blender
- Teaspoon
- 1½ cups of dry roasted peanuts
- Stopwatch

WHAT YOU DO

1. Ask an adult to help you blend the dry roasted peanuts and honey for 60 seconds. Taste a little and note the texture.
2. Add oil and blend until smooth and creamy.
3. Taste a little and note the texture. Add a little oil if the mixture seems too dry.
4. Cool the mixture in a fridge for two hours.

QUIZ QUESTION:

WHAT WILL HAPPEN TO THE MIXTURE AT STEP 4?

A) IT BECOMES SOFT AND RUNNY

B) IT GETS THICK AND HARD

C) IT SLOWLY TURNS GREEN

WHAT HAPPENS?

ANSWER: B

This experiment is about mixing and changing materials. Blending breaks up the plant **cells**, releasing peanut oil that mixes with sunflower oil and honey. Cooling oil molecules form clumps that thicken the mixture.

DID YOU KNOW?

Peanuts aren't technically nuts because they don't grow on trees. They're more closely related to beans or peas and grow underground.

CRAZY SODA

Sodas are bad for you, but they reveal an amazing, bubbly secret . . . .

WHAT YOU NEED

Glass

Brand-new empty spray bottle

Can of soda

WHAT YOU DO

1. Wash the spray bottle with soapy water. Fill with water.
2. Open the soda and pour it into a glass.
3. Wait for the soda to stop bubbling and then spray it with water.
4. Do not drink the soda—pour it all out!

WARNING!
ONLY USE A BRAND-NEW AND EMPTY SPRAY BOTTLE. OTHERS MAY CONTAIN HARMFUL CHEMICALS.

QUIZ QUESTION:

WHAT WILL HAPPEN TO THE SODA?

A) IT FIZZES UP

B) IT MAKES A LOUD BURPING NOISE

C) IT GLOWS IN THE DARK

WHAT HAPPENS?

ANSWER: A

To make a soda, carbon dioxide is forced into the drink under pressure. Soda contains dissolved carbon dioxide gas.

The spray pushes air into the soda. The air forms bubbles and the dissolved carbon dioxide gas enters the bubbles. The bubbles get bigger, and they rise and pop with a fizzing sound.

WHAT'S NEXT?

Try the same experiment with flat (non-bubbly) soda. Does it still work—if not, why?

MAKE MICROBE FIZZ

They may be impossible to see with the naked eye, but microbes are everywhere!

WHAT YOU NEED

WHAT YOU DO

1. Ask an adult to boil two cups of water in the saucepan. Stir in $\frac{1}{3}$ of a tablespoon of ground ginger, $\frac{1}{3}$ cup of sugar, and one tablespoon of lemon juice.
2. Cover the pan and leave on the heat until the mixture is warm.
3. Stir in $\frac{1}{3}$ of a teaspoon of yeast. Replace the lid and leave for two hours with the heat off.
4. Sift the mixture into the jug. Using the funnel, pour the liquid into the bottle until it's $2\frac{1}{2}$ inches from the top. Screw the cap tightly onto the bottle.
5. Leave in the fridge for at least twelve hours. When you can't press the bottle in, it's ready to be opened slowly.

QUIZ QUESTION:

WHAT WILL MAKE THE FIZZ?

A) A CHEMICAL REACTION BETWEEN LEMON JUICE AND SUGAR

B) THE YEAST

C) MICROBES IN THE GINGER

WARNING!

DO NOT LEAVE IN THE FRIDGE FOR MORE THAN 36 HOURS. DO NOT DRINK THE EXPERIMENT!

ANSWER: B

Yeasts are microscopic fungi. Unlike animals, yeasts can live without oxygen. They produce carbon dioxide by chemically transforming sugars. You can probably hear the gas fizzing during Step 3.

WHAT HAPPENS?

MAKING SOLUTIONS

Heat energy doesn't just get water moving. It affects chemical reactions, too . . . .

WHAT YOU NEED

WHAT YOU DO

1. Fill the jug with water and add some ice cubes.
2. Leave the water jug to chill in the fridge for two hours. Add one cup of hot water to one glass and one cup of cold water from the fridge to the other glass.
3. Using separate spoons, add one teaspoonful of salt to each glass. Stir well to dissolve as much salt as you can.

QUIZ QUESTION:

WHERE WILL THE SALT DISSOLVE BEST?

A) HOT WATER

B) COLD WATER

C) NEITHER—BUT THE COLD GLASS STARTS TO STEAM

WHAT HAPPENS?

ANSWER: A

Water molecules pull the salt crystal particles apart for the salt to dissolve. At a higher temperature, the water molecules move faster and hit the crystals more often. This dissolves the salt crystals more quickly.

WHAT'S NEXT?

Try using sugar instead of salt. Does sugar dissolve more easily? If so, why?

FLOATING WATER

This great experiment adds heat energy to water with colorful results.

WHAT YOU NEED

1½ fl oz. bottle

Deep clear jug of water

Liquid food coloring (not gel)

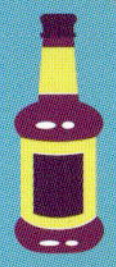

WHAT YOU DO

1. Leave the jug of water in the fridge for a few hours.
2. Add a few drops of coloring to the small bottle and then top it off with hot tap water.
3. Place the small bottle at the bottom of the larger jug.

WARNING!
ASK AN ADULT FOR HELP WHEN USING HOT WATER IN EXPERIMENTS.

QUIZ QUESTION:

WHAT WILL HAPPEN?

A) THE HOT WATER RISES UP

B) NOTHING—HOT AND COLD WATER DON'T MIX

C) THE BOTTLE WILL EXPLODE

COLD WATER SINKS

HOT WATER RISES

WHAT HAPPENS?

ANSWER: A

Heat energy makes the molecules in the water move faster and farther apart. This makes the water expand and become less dense than cold water. The hot water rises and the colder, denser water sinks to fill the gap.

WHAT'S NEXT?

Leave the experiment for an hour. What happens to the hot water? Why?

DID YOU KNOW?

When you are boiling water in a kettle, the source of the heat is at the bottom. The water at the bottom heats and rises to the top of the kettle. The cooler water that has not yet been heated sinks to the bottom of the kettle for its turn to be warmed.

GAS BALLOON

Our atmosphere consists of all sorts of different gases. Here's an easy scientific way to make your own.

WHAT YOU DO

1. Use the funnel to add two teaspoonfuls of baking powder to the bottle. Rinse the funnel with water.
2. Use the funnel to fill the second balloon up to its neck with vinegar.
3. Stretch the balloon over the bottle's neck, but don't allow any vinegar into the bottle just yet.
4. Place the bottle in a sink and lift the balloon so that the vinegar pours into the bottle.
5. Watch the balloon inflate and then tie the end. Blow up the second balloon so it is the same size as the first balloon. Compare the weight of both balloons in your hands.

WHAT YOU NEED

QUIZ QUESTION:

WHICH BALLOON IS HEAVIER?

A) THE CONTROL BALLOON

B) THE BALLOON FROM THE BOTTLE

C) THEY BOTH WEIGH THE SAME

WHAT HAPPENS?

ANSWER: B

The balloon fills with carbon dioxide gas from a reaction between baking powder and vinegar.

The heavier-than-air gas makes the balloon a little heavier than an identical balloon containing the same amount of air.

DID YOU KNOW?

Plants use carbon dioxide gas, water, and sunlight to make food in their leaves. This is called **photosynthesis**.

GLOSSARY

Air pressure
The force of the air pressing on something. Air pressure increases with temperature.

Atom
A particle made up of a nucleus (containing protons and neutrons), usually surrounded by electrons. It's hard to break atoms into smaller particles.

Cell
Living unit that makes up larger life-forms. Cells can divide to make more cells.

Density
The mass of a certain volume of a substance.

Dissolves
When a solid breaks into smaller particles in a liquid, such as water.

Indicator
Substances that change color when they are added to acidic or alkaline solutions.

Mass
The matter (atoms, etc.) that makes up an object.

Molecule
A group of atoms joined together. They can form or break up in chemical reactions.

Photosynthesis
The way green plants make sugar from carbon dioxide and water using energy from light.

Polymers
Molecule formed from lots of smaller molecules arranged in a chain.

Surface tension
Surfaces of liquids such as water are springy because the molecules are slightly drawn together.

INDEX

PICTURE CREDITS

(t=top, b=bottom, l=left, r=right, c=center)

Shutterstock

7 verca, 8b meunierd, 8b oksana2010, 9b Nikola Bilic, 11c Robyn Mackenzie, 13t Dmitrydesign, 15b NAAN, 16b Giancarlo Liguori, 17b Fernando Sanchez Cortes, 21b SJ Travel Photo and Video, 22 Greg Brave.